Creating Requirements for Software Projects: A Business Analyst's Guide to Requirements Management

Table of Contents

3

Creating Requirements for Software Projects: A Business Analyst's Guide to Requirements Management

ISBN 978-0-9878245-6-1
Published by Writer Types Inc., Kingston, Ontario, Canada

Dedication

To my husband and partner, Tarek Hussein, who has dedicated his life to helping others.

Introduction

When I began writing requirements 20 years ago, I really didn't have a solid idea about what requirements were. What was a good requirement? What was a bad requirement? Was my requirement complete? There were no clear standards I could find, nor was there anybody around I could ask. After all, it was my job, not anybody else's.

I muddled my way through the project, which was to obtain an IT solution to manage $2 billion per year. It seemed that my team, which included IT, business, and legal stakeholders, were happy with the result. This was really the only indicator of quality that I had at the time. When we issued the Request for Proposal (RFP), I then received some more feedback about the requirements. The global vendors (which included Microsoft® as a partner) said the RFP was "one of the best RFPs" they had ever seen. Now, I was beaming about how great my requirements were.

My pride suffered a setback when the project was awarded and the vendor was onboarded. It became clear that my requirements could've been better. There was too much "wiggle room" in terms of how the words could've been interpreted, which led to some squabbling with the vendor. In addition, not all of the requirements were written with the lens of how they could've been tested. As I later learned, you might write a great requirement, but if you can't write and execute a test for it, how do you know it's been implemented correctly?

Many years after this experience, I learned the formal methods of requirements elicitation and management developed by the International Institute of Business Analysis™ (IIBA®). I obtained the Certified Business Analysis Professional™ (CBAP®) certification and also graduated from a university program in business analysis. I plunged into business analysis books and gleaned websites in order to understand business analysis in depth.

Today, leveraging my background as a college instructor and business analysis consultant I teach others about requirements. In this book, I attempted to impart this knowledge in a practical, streamlined way with lived experience in order to give you a "shortcut" to understanding the IIBA methodology and approach as found in *A Guide to the Business Analysis Body of Knowledge® (the BABOK® Guide)*. My hope is that you find this information useful in your own business analysis work.

What This Book Isn't

This book isn't everything you need. It's a beginner's guide to get you started in the world of requirements. To become a high-caliber business analyst, I'd recommend becoming a member of IIBA and memorizing the *BABOK® Guide.* I'd also recommend taking formal courses in business analysis from an IIBA-endorsed educational provider (I prefer post-secondary institutions because that's what is generally asked for in job postings). Further, I'd suggest hanging out with other business analysts to learn the latest trends, hear what challenges they have in their jobs and how they solve them, and plug into the community. While this book isn't everything you need, it does encompass the perspective of one business analyst's career over 20 years—the good, the bad, and the other.

How to Use This Book

Read this book from beginning to end. Don't jump around and read it out of order. Disregard the parts that don't apply to you. Remember as you're reading that the content represents my own perspectives, not that of any organization, and your opinions and experience may differ. Business analysis is a big world with lots of room for variation.

Before You Begin Your New Project

Suppose you've been assigned to an IT project and you've been asked by the business to do requirements for a new IT solution. This means you're the "glue" between IT and the business. You're the master of requirements. What do you need to know? To do? Who do you talk to? What processes do you set up? It can seem so overwhelming in the beginning if you're new to writing IT requirements, but there is a logical place for you to start—it's with the *BABOK® Guide.*

The *BABOK® Guide* is the international standard in business analysis. Rather than repeat its excellent content (as many business analysis books do), I'll refer you to the *BABOK® Guide* as necessary. No book I've ever

read has beat the comprehensiveness of the *BABOK®
Guide* (which was a factor in me latte-pricing this book,
so you could also budget for the *BABOK® Guide*),
although one fair criticism of the book is that it's
theoretical and doesn't provide day-to-day practical tips
that business analysts can use on IT projects. If you don't
already have the guide, it's available to members on the
IIBA website (iiba.org) and major book and eBook
retailers.

Rather than read the entire *BABOK® Guide* (which is a
beast in page count, as big as a woolly mammoth), for
the purposes of understanding this book on requirements,
I'd recommend reading—actually, inhaling—the specific
parts of the *BABOK® Guide* that I've identified below
prior to reading this book. I'll be discussing these parts
in more detail throughout the book. Pay special attention
to the following sections:

Requirements classification schema: This section
defines the different types of requirements, including
business, stakeholder, solution (both functional and non-
functional), and transition. Know the differences
between these requirement types and how they're used
on your project. I'd recommended searching for every
instance of these terms throughout the *BABOK® Guide*
and collating your understanding from these collective
references for a holistic perspective.

Requirements and designs: I'll discuss in more detail
why it's critical to know the difference between
requirements and designs, and how this will shape your

requirements efforts. For now, read this section just to understand the basic difference.

Business analysis planning and monitoring: This section in the *BABOK® Guide* is very comprehensive in its theoretical approach to planning and monitoring business analysis activities. If you understand the high-level concepts (meaning the definitions of approach, stakeholder engagement, governance, information management, and performance improvements), that's enough for the deep dive that I'll do in my book. Don't spend too much time here.

Elicitation and collaboration: This section in the *BABOK® Guide* is really key to your job in requirements. Again, it's likely more thorough and theoretical than you need for your projects, but since it's central to requirements activities, read it well.

Requirements Life Cycle Management (RLCM): I love that the *BABOK® Guide* has included an entire chapter on RLCM, as I find that it's one of the most overlooked areas when creating and managing requirements, mostly because the business analyst or project team lack understanding of the importance of doing so; however, not attending to RLCM can cause unpredictable headaches and delays on your project.

Strategy analysis: I find that strategy analysis is another area where stakeholders tend not to understand the importance of in the same way that business analysts should. Read this section at a high level to understand the concepts of needs, current state, future state, risk identification, and change strategy.

Requirements Analysis and Design Definition (RADD): This is a key section from the *BABOK® Guide* for your requirements tasks, but like other parts of the *BABOK® Guide*, you only need to understand it at a high level because I've "drilled down" for you later on. Just know the main concepts of specify and model requirements, verify requirements, validate requirements, and define requirements architecture.

While the other information in the *BABOK® Guide* is good to know (especially if you plan to take an IIBA certification exam), in this book about requirements only the above sections are required reading. I'd recommend that you read these sections first before proceeding further.

What Is a Requirement?

"Requirement" is a term that is used in a multitude of ways by many people and industries. For business analysts, requirements are known to "address a need" which sounds, in my view, too abstract. For now, all you need to know is that a requirement is something that somebody else needs.

You know this in your daily life. I need food. I need my coffee in the morning. I need my car to start. I need money to pay my bills. I need my phone to turn on so I can make calls to clients. I need these requirements for daily living.

For an IT solution, let's say a music app, a user needs to create a profile, log in, create a playlist, share music, and so on. That's what the users need in order to enjoy the music app. Each of these items is a requirement.

Let's also consider an online banking system. When users do online banking, they need to log in, check account balances, pay bills, order cheques, and so on. This functionality, called solution requirements (and even more specifically, functional solution requirements), is what they need in order to do online banking. By the way, there are other requirement types involved in an online banking system. Requirements about the "backend" of a system—the response time, speed, and so on—are called non-functional solution requirements. We'll learn more about these and other types of requirements when discussing requirement types.

What Do I Do First?

I'm often asked what a business analyst should do first on a project. There are so many tasks that *could* be done first that it may be difficult for you to figure out what you *should* do. This is completely understandable, especially if you're hired by an organization that has never worked with a business analyst before. They may have no business analysis tools or processes, or even an understanding of what you need to do your work.

From my perspective, the first thing you should do is read. Yes. True. Read everything you can get your hands on, starting with documents about the project and organization. Read their sales and marketing collateral, presentations to executives, and technical documents. Google the organization and read media stories about them. Research current IT solutions in the industry and understand the functionality available in these solutions. Turn over every stone and talk to everybody you can. An unexpected source of information on one of my projects was the university intern who shared my workspace. Read until you feel like you've ingested a huge bowl of soup and you just can't have one more spoonful.

After you've filled up on reading material, then do your own assessment of what tools and processes they have. Figure out what you have and don't have (and need). In consultation with your stakeholders, strive to understand their project vision and goals, what a successful project looks like to them, and any preferred ways of working. You never know—sometimes an "obvious" stakeholder preference isn't so obvious to an external consultant. On one project I worked on, the project manager wanted a mini-status every week. On another project, they never read my weekly status reports and didn't notice them missing when I stopped sending them—the project manager was only interested in hearing about the problems as they occurred and would lend their support as needed.

For a new music app project, especially in a fast-paced start-up company, there might only be a minimal amount of company documentation so rely on other sources, competitor and industry websites and discussion groups.

Where Project Management Intersects

As a business analyst on an IT project, you'll likely be doing your business analysis tasks within an overall project management framework led by a project manager. It's imperative that you understand how your business analyst work fits into, and is affected by, the project management framework since as a project team everybody works together. While several different project management methodologies exist, generally the phases are similar to the following:

Project Management Phases		
🚀	Initiation	-Identify business need, problem, or opportunity -Determine project feasibility -Create business case -Identity scope, deliverables, and stakeholders
📅	Planning	-Create project plan -Estimate budget -Build team
🏃	Execution	-Build IT solution -Manage team and work tasks -Provide status and updates -Manage budget and schedule -Manage project changes
🏋	Closure	-Analyze planned schedule, budget, and scope versus actual -Conduct post-implementation reviews -Close project

In terms of your role, you may be requested to help the project manager with project management deliverables during any of these phases, from initiation through to closure, in addition to doing your own business analyst deliverables such as requirements. Further still, sometimes the line between the two disciplines is blurred, and deliverables such as the business case can be completed by the project manager, business analyst, or somebody else.

Within each of these project management phases, you'll be doing business analysis tasks according to the IIBA business analysis knowledge areas (and of course, your stakeholders' specifications!). The two models don't fit together seamlessly (and they're not meant to, they've been developed separately by two different disciplines), but over time and experience you'll learn where you need to plug into the project management phases. Let's take a look at the *BABOK® Guide* knowledge areas, then fit the two models together.

Business Analysis Knowledge Areas	
Business Analysis Planning and Monitoring	Plan business analysis approach Plan stakeholder engagement Plan business analysis governance Plan business analysis information management Identify business analysis performance improvements
Strategy Analysis	Analyze current state Define future state Assess risks Define change strategy

Business Analysis Knowledge Areas	
Elicitation and Collaboration	Prepare for elicitation Conduct elicitation Confirm elicitation results Communication business analysis information Manage stakeholder collaboration
Requirements Analysis and Design Definition (RADD)	Specify and model requirements Verify requirements Validate requirements Define requirements architecture Define design options Analyze potential value and recommend solution
Requirements Life Cycle Management (RLCM)	Trace requirements Maintain requirements Prioritize requirements Assess requirements changes Approve requirements
Solution Evaluation	Measure solution performance Analyze performance measures Assess solution limitations Assess enterprise limitations Recommend actions to increase solution value

In project management, notice that the phases are done sequentially (with some exceptions, which we don't need to get into). First you need to first initiate a project, then do the planning. Next, you can do the execution phase where you build the IT solution, and finally you would close the project as the last phase. This makes sense. We certainly wouldn't close the project before we started it!

Key point: *Whereas project management phases are done in a sequential order, business analysis knowledge areas are done in a concurrent manner.* As an example, we need information from our stakeholders on an ongoing basis throughout the project in order to complete our deliverables (this is the elicitation and collaboration knowledge area). This makes sense, right? We talk to our stakeholders all the time to plan our approach, develop strategy, elicit requirements, define the life cycle of our requirements, and evaluate the solution; therefore, elicitation and collaboration doesn't occur once in a prescribed order but occurs concurrently as we progress through our project. That being said, you can generally expect, in terms of knowledge areas, that planning and monitoring will occur mainly in the beginning of your work along with strategy analysis, then RLCM and RADD, and solution evaluation at the end.

In terms of mapping the *BABOK® Guide* knowledge areas to project management phases, to speak specifically to requirements (since that's the focus of this book), while it's possible to begin eliciting requirements in the initiation and planning phases, especially if you're helping the project manager complete the business case, more often than not, business analysts do the bulk of their work in the planning and execution phases, while doing a minimal amount of work in the closure phase. Of course, we cannot be so prescriptive as timing varies across projects and organizations.

As already mentioned, these business analysis knowledge areas do not fit neatly into the project management phases, so it's best to identify your business analysis deliverables at the beginning of your project and work in close consultation with the project manager to understand how you can support his project management phases.

Get Your Head Around Strategy Analysis

This book isn't about strategy analysis; however, in order to understand how to create and manage requirements, you'll need to understand what strategy analysis is and how it impacts requirements creation.

As the *BABOK® Guide* indicates, strategy analysis refers to a set of tasks that you do primarily at the beginning of the project that identifies the business need and solution scope. The need may be "a new proposal management IT solution" or a "new billing IT solution." Typically, the need would've been identified by project leaders long before you're onboarded as a business analyst.

Sometimes, work has been going on for many years by others until you're onboarded. Perhaps the executive already identified the need for a new IT solution in response to a new government regulation or a new program. Or, maybe an auditor found some major deficiencies that would be fixed by new functionality. In any case, management would likely have a project manager in place who wrote a project charter (or similar document). The project charter identifies the resources needed, estimated timelines, deliverables, and so forth. Maybe the business case has already been completed, or you'll be asked to do that.

When you're onboarded as a business analyst, it's key to find out the *why*. Why is a new IT solution needed, and what is the problem or opportunity that will be addressed? Here are some typical reasons why an IT solution is needed:

- Current IT solution is near obsolete and uses outdated technology that can't be supported by the IT department.
- New government regulations and safety standards in aircraft necessitated improvements to an existing IT solution.
- A new grants and contributions program requires a new IT solution be built to manage $750 million of federal funds.
- Customers were unhappy with the previous release and it didn't meet expectations.

In any case, to do strategy analysis with your stakeholders, you'll need to analyze the current state, define the future state, identify risks, and then define the change strategy, just as the *BABOK® Guide* indicates (this is another time where the *BABOK® Guide* does a great job, so why repeat it?). If you analyze "current state and future state" in terms of "people, process, and technology" you'll have a great idea what your project is about.

For "people" you can ask the following questions, at a minimum:
- Which resources are involved in current state? In future state?
- Do resources need to be increased or decreased from current state to future state?
- Do resources need to be reallocated to other locations?
- Do resources need training or any new capabilities to enable future state?
- Are there any corporate culture changes required to enable future state?
- Are there any other changes needed from current state to future state?

For "process" you can ask the following questions, at a minimum:
- Are current processes and future processes documented? (If they're not documented, then you need to do them. Refer to good resources on process development to assist you.)
- How do current processes need to be changed to enable future state? Do they need to be improved or redesigned?
- Are there any current manual processes, and will any be automated in the future state (in the new IT solution)?

For "technology" you can ask the following questions, at a minimum:

- How are tools and technologies changing from current state to future state? (Which existing ones are being kept as is, modified, or replaced?)
- What other technologies/systems are impacted by this IT solution? Will any of them need to change for the future state?
- What are the data requirements for this project, and how is current state different from future state?

You could depict "people, process and technology" for "current state and future state" using a variety of techniques. I've chosen to present it as a graphic:

Current State		

People

20 personnel	Departments: accounting, program, data	Process applications manually

Process

Monitor program process	Approve funding process	Distribute funding process
Assess application process	Evaluation application process	
Manual processes only		

Technology

No online system	Applicant applies by email only
Application progress tracked in Excel	Personnel save applicant files manually to network drive

Future State		

People

| 20 personnel | Departments: accounting, program, data | Process applications in new system |

Training on new system required

Process

Monitor program process	Approve funding process	Distribute funding process
Assess application process	Evaluation application process	
All processes online, none manual	Processes need to be re-engineered for online use	

Technology

| No manual processing | Applicant applies through new system |
| Application progress tracked in system | All files stored in new system |

As the *BABOK® Guide* indicates, after you've identified the current state and future state, you'll want to do a gap analysis to determine how you can move from current state to future state, and also create your change strategy. You'll also want to identify all of the risks involved. The risks I encounter on IT projects are typically the common ones relating to scope, budget, and timelines. Refer to the *BABOK® Guide* for more information about these topics, as the scope of this book is dedicated to requirements. With strategy analysis now complete, you have the business requirements and the high-level picture of the project that you need in order to create requirements for the new IT solution.

Understand Your Assignment

It might sound obvious when I say that you need to understand your assignment. Yet, how many times have we heard "this isn't what I wanted"? Maybe we have even said it ourselves. I know that I've had those feelings in restaurants, sinking my teeth into the first bite of a delicious-looking dinner and saying, "That's not what I wanted at all."

If you understand the project, you can begin to better understand your assignment. It's really critical that you understand where you fit into the project—what you're expected to do versus what others are expected to do—because there's the possibility that some of the requirements, or tasks related to requirements, have already been done by others. Don't assume that you need to implement end-to-end "perfect" business analysis.

Sometimes, there can be titanic discrepancies in opinions about the role of the business analyst. Perhaps this is due to assumptions or a lack of understanding. Whatever the reason, it's your job as a business analyst to understand your assignment and also ensure that your stakeholders understand your role and what you need from them. Outline your tasks, deliverables, and timelines, and communicate your process and approach so stakeholders understand more of your world.

For one project, I was tasked with creating requirements for a new government IT solution. My stakeholder was an engineer, but didn't have exposure to IT projects. He couldn't understand why requirements took so long to create. Why couldn't we just do the requirements on an electronic whiteboard, take a picture, and send them to IT to create our IT solution? It sounded like a few days of work.

Using only an electronic whiteboard to create and maintain requirements would cause a lot of issues, beginning with the lack of control over the content. Any member of the team could have access to and inadvertently change the requirement (so we wouldn't have any traceability). We would never know if somebody changed or deleted any requirement because the whiteboard didn't keep a history of changes.

In addition, the content in the whiteboard was not easily shareable, so we couldn't email it to others or import it into documents. Further, the whiteboard lacked the capability to sort and filter requirements. Over time and hundreds of requirements later, it would've been very difficult to find what we're looking for. Nevertheless, it wasn't the stakeholder's fault for wanting an electronic whiteboard. It was up to me as the business analyst on the project to educate the stakeholder about possible negative outcomes of using the wrong tool to maintain requirements.

Take the time to understand exactly what your stakeholders want you to do, educate as necessary, and have a clear understanding about what your deliverables are, the tools you'll use to create the deliverables, and your timelines. Your stakeholders also need the same understanding of your work so you get the proper support.

For the music app project, let's say that you're asked to create the requirements for this app and you're the first business analyst the company has ever hired. This means that part of your assignment will need to be setting up a business analyst department with templates, processes, and standards. In another company where there is a department of dedicated business analysts, your assignment may only be to create requirements using the existing templates.

Fit Into Your Environment

As a consultant, I've worked for about 50 organizations. I can tell you with surety that every organization was different from the other. Different products and services.

Different processes and procedures. Different personalities. Different corporate culture. Different ways to get things done. Different measures of success and productivity. What one organization considered "friendly negotiation" another organization labelled as too assertive (or something worse). As a consultant, I can't bring in a "templated" way of working and blindly apply it to an environment. Bad idea.

One of the first things I do is get to know the organization at every level, beginning with the people. I keep my eyes and ears open for how they interact with each other and then respect that. If they speak indirectly and in nuanced ways, meaning the statement "there are other ways to do things" actually means "don't do it this way" then I pay attention to that. Your project will only be as successful as your relationships within that organization—it's the people who give you the information, approvals, and all the rest of the knowledge you need to have a successful project.

What might be a good requirement in one stakeholder's eyes is unfeasible in another's eyes. Business stakeholders might give you a requirement they anticipate will bring in more revenue for the organization, but when you put the same requirement in front of the IT stakeholders, they tell you it isn't technically feasible. Or it's technically feasible but would require that they hire 5 developers to implement it. Or, suppose the business and IT stakeholders like the requirement, but the project manager concludes that it will take too much time and interfere with the overall project schedule. So, know who your stakeholders are and ensure that you have proper representation in your requirements workshops. One of the worst things that can happen to a business analyst is to have "final" requirements that have been reviewed by the wrong stakeholders, or an incomplete group of stakeholders.

If you know your environment well, and the people in it, you'll be able to identify who the key influencers are, and how much weight their ideas carry in the organization. If they have a high level of influence and impact with respect to your project, I'd consider their comments more carefully than somebody who has a low level of influence and impact.

Suppose for the music app, the company is a small start-up, which is a small, newly formed technology company. Start-ups are known for certain traits, including immature processes, insufficient documentation, "flat" organizations lacking a complex hierarchy, and a fast-paced, quickly changing environment. It's not uncommon for personnel to be doing multiple roles at the same time (for example, business analyst and technical writer) and working long hours including evenings and weekends. Approval processes may be expedited and informal, and could include a hallway conversation or a drink after work. The start-up may not even have a formal documentation management system. In terms of stakeholders, it might seem that the few loud extroverts who dominate the requirements workshops are the key players, but then the business analyst notices that the "quiet guy" in the room—the software architect—is the only person who successfully overturns their decisions. Even the CEO turns to the software architect for advice. A diligent business analyst will recognize company dynamics and organize their time and attention with stakeholders accordingly. Know your environment and fit into it.

Identify the Software Development Methodology

Identify the software development methodology used on the project. Is the organization using a predictive approach like Waterfall or an adaptive approach like Agile? Or a hybrid of the two? There are several, and it's your responsibility as a business analyst to know which software development methodology the organization is using and how that affects your work.

Understand the developers' process so you can plug into it and supply them with requirements in the right format at the time they need. Make sense? If you don't understand the software development methodology they're using, then you may supply requirements that aren't in the right structure, don't contain the right information, or are too late or too early (both scenarios can be problematic for different reasons). Consider the developers as key stakeholders who you need to understand and help.

Suppose in the music app project, the developers uses an Agile-like methodology. The developers don't use Agile in its strictest sense, but use bits and pieces of Agile that suit them at this early stage of their company's maturity. They have a product backlog (which is akin to a "to do" list of user stories to code as functionality) they use to continually reprioritize requirements for development, but then the developers also make changes without telling the business analyst because they're just focused on getting the app done, not necessarily on team communication. They have daily scrum meetings (daily stand-ups) to review progress updates then also text each other throughout the night as they furiously pound away at their keyboards churning out code. In this environment, not only does the business analyst need to understand Agile, but she also needs to know what parts of Agile the start-up has thrown out.

So, get to know the developers. Make friends with them. This is a key factor in successful projects.

Launch Your Business Analysis Tools

Some organizations already have requirements management tools that you can use. (If this is the case, it's a positive indication that they also have familiarity with business analysis, at least to some degree. Whew.) Other organizations may have these requirements management tools but don't have licenses for consultants, so you won't be using them. Still other organizations don't have any tools at all, so you'll be using Microsoft Office and whatever you can get for free. When I'm using Microsoft Office as my tools, here's how I do it:

Microsoft PowerPoint

On a project I develop presentations for a variety of reasons, which may include:

- **Project overview:** Before I begin my requirements workshops, I always provide a project overview to ensure that all stakeholders have the same understanding about scope, timelines, goals of the project, roles and responsibilities, and so on.

- **Functionality overview:** Before the new IT solution is released, typically I provide stakeholders a functionality overview so they know which functionality was implemented in the upcoming release and which functionality was deferred. In addition, if some desired functionality had to be deleted, I may include this information in the presentation or speak privately to the interested stakeholder(s) prior to the presentation.

- **Risks:** Sometimes I encounter risks where I need input from stakeholders. Suppose the developers determined that a requirement would need twice the amount of time to implement than originally thought, which may cause a risk to the schedule. I need to ensure that key stakeholders are aware of this risk so I outline the situation, the impact and probability of the risk, and the pros and cons of proceeding on course so they can make an informed decision.

- **Decisions:** It's happened to all of us—stakeholders who stand their ground and can't agree, which stalls our requirements process. Trying to make them budge is like trying to move a grizzly off a picnic table. In these kinds of situations, if facilitation and negotiation fails, I may create a presentation about the options available and outline the various scenarios and impacts for the key stakeholders to decide. Usually, it's the highest-ranking person in the room who decides the outcome.

Microsoft Visio or Lucid Software's Lucidchart
I use Microsoft Visio to create processes and diagrams. Alternately, I use Lucid Software's Lucidchart, which is an online alternative to Visio.

Microsoft Word
I use Microsoft Word for general documents, taking notes, requirements workshops, and so on.

Microsoft Project
If I'm creating a schedule for my business analyst deliverables to give to the project manager, I'll do it in Microsoft Project. Alternately, on a simple project, I may just do my schedule in Excel.

Microsoft Excel
In the absence of a dedicated requirements management tool, I use Microsoft Excel to create my requirements matrix. It works "good enough" to sort and filter columns and share with stakeholders, unlike dedicated requirements management tools that may require expensive licensing. I generally include the following columns:

- **Number:** This is the original row number. I use this column to resort the rows back to the original order after I've "sliced and diced" the data for different views.

- **Requirement number:** This is an alphanumeric value to easily identify the requirement. I may use a simple structure like REQ-1, REQ-2, REQ-3. I may also further identify the requirement based on module; for example, for an invoicing module, I might use INV-4, INV-5, and INV-6 to identify the requirement.
- **Priority:** Is the requirement a low, medium, or high priority for stakeholders? Best to have that flagged, which can be particularly useful in discussions about scope.
- **Category:** This is the major category for the requirement. I like the category column because I've noticed that stakeholders provide requirements based on categories; for example, the project management stakeholders give me requirements about project management and the accountants give me requirements about billing. It's just another nice category to have in sorting and filtering requirements.
- **Title:** This is the title of the requirement. Every requirement needs a short title.
- **Requirement:** This is the requirement itself. Be sure to write the requirement in the format your organization prefers (for my projects, this has mainly been the Agile format of user story and acceptance criteria). Check with your organization about their preferred requirement format.
- **Version:** This is the version of the IT solution the requirement will be implemented in. I have worked in environments that didn't have official versions

(which sounds surprising even to me), so I worked with the developers to create them.

- **Version date:** This is the date the version (from the previous column) is ready for user acceptance testing (UAT).
- **Status:** This is the current status of the requirement; for example, draft, reviewed, approved, UAT-tested, and implemented.
- **Date:** This is the date of the current status (from the previous column).
- **Notes:** Every spreadsheet needs a notes column, right? My own notes go here, as well as notes from meetings, emails from stakeholders, and so on that I need to refer to or that's important to keep with the requirement. I continually populate the notes column with changes and considerations. My notes contain the date, comment (either a change, risk or other type of information), and the person who provided the comment.
- **IT feedback:** This is a running column of IT feedback on the specific requirement, which has proven to be very useful when managing hundreds of requirements and a stakeholder asks me IT's feedback on a specific requirement.

Other Tools

While not officially a "tool," I also take a lot of photos—of meeting notes on a whiteboard, screen mockups that I draw by hand and want to share with stakeholders, and defects I discover in the prototype. Photos are easy, fast, and portable. Just make sure that you're not violating any of the organization's privacy or ethics policies.

Blastoff Your Business Analysis Processes

Along with your business analysis tools, you'll also need to establish your business analysis processes. This book isn't specifically about business analysis processes, but for information here are some of the common ones that I'll discuss in more detail throughout the book:

Requirements elicitation process: In order to create a requirements elicitation process, you first need to understand what it is, so read the *BABOK® Guide*. Then, for your project, address the following questions: How are you getting the information to create requirements? Who can you interview, either inside of the organization or in the industry? What kind of workshops will you conduct and who will you invite?

Requirements Life Cycle Management (RLCM) process: In order to create a RLCM process, you first need to understand what it is, so read the *BABOK® Guide*. Then, for your project, address the following questions: How are you drafting, reviewing, and updating your requirements? How are you communicating these changes? How are you keeping track of changes made, by who, and when? When I don't have formal requirements management tools and I'm using Microsoft Excel, I make sure that I'm the only one who has the ability to change a master copy of the requirements matrix, and request others to either submit their changes by email or clearly indicate their updates in their own version of the matrix.

Stakeholder management process: Are you surprised that I suggest you have a stakeholder management process? For business analysts, stakeholders are everything! We need them. We need to know how to engage them, elicit information from them, and hone those relationships for the future. I have lots of techniques that I use for stakeholder management, and some of them are included in this book. I might write another book about stakeholders. Hmm. Maybe.

Document management process: Many years ago, I wrote a book about how to manage documentation projects for a course I was teaching at a Toronto college. There's so much to know about managing documentation, and it's not only about keeping track of versions. If you would like a free copy of this book, connect with me on Twitter @pampaterson and I'll send you a copy. Alternatively, read business analysis books that are dedicated to project management.

Project management process: Shouldn't project management be the responsibility of the project manager? Yes and no. The project manager is responsible for the overall project, but every team member also has an individual responsibility to implement a subset of project management processes for their respective areas. For business analysts, you need to be mindful of scope and timelines, at a minimum. You also need to be attentive to risks and dependencies. Ideally, you're sending a "clean" status to the project manager when requested because you've handled everything at your level. If you have any concerns that you can't handle, such as lack of available information or cooperation, then you should quickly escalate these to the project manager.

Determine Your Business Analysis Techniques

A business analysis technique is a method you use to do business analysis work. The *BABOK® Guide* has the most comprehensive list of techniques I've ever seen. I counted about 50 before my eyes got tired. You'll use these techniques throughout the project, sometimes multiple times; for example, you'll use the interview technique throughout the project for different purposes, such as planning, requirements elicitation, and so on. You may be interviewing project executives in the beginning about their goals, then interviewing other stakeholders to elicit requirements. You may use the backlog management technique to manage requirements. You may need the glossary technique so stakeholders understand the terminology used in your requirements. And on and on it goes. I love these techniques and enjoy spending time selecting the ones I need for a project. Business analysts have their favorites, and often use the same ones over and over. Here are some of the techniques I use most often:

- Acceptance and evaluation criteria
- Backlog management
- Brainstorming
- Business cases
- Business rules analysis
- Data dictionary

- Data flow diagrams
- Decision analysis
- Document analysis
- Glossary
- Interviews
- Lessons learned
- Prioritization
- Process modelling
- Prototyping
- Reviews
- Roles and permissions matrix
- Scope modelling
- Stakeholder list, map, or personas
- State modelling
- Use cases and scenarios
- User stories
- Vendor assessment
- Workshops

The *BABOK® Guide* explains the theoretical perspective of these techniques very clearly, and I'd also recommend finding examples so you can see them in practice. There are lots of examples online.

Requirements Versus Designs

Before we dive into requirements, it's important to understand the difference between requirements and designs, essentially because the business analyst is mainly responsible for requirements while the developers are primarily accountable for the design of the solution.

What happens if you don't know the difference, and you're doing design instead of requirements? The developers may get very frustrated with you. Know that the developers can't move forward with their designing tasks if you don't have the requirements done. What could they code if they don't have requirements? And they don't need you to design the solution for them, anyway—this is their expertise.

The basic difference between requirements and design is that requirements represent "what a stakeholder needs" and design represents "how that need will be delivered." As the *BABOK® Guide* says, "requirements are focused on the need; designs are focused on the solution."

As an example, let's suppose stakeholders say, "We need applicants to be able to send us legal documents in a secure manner." That's the requirement. That's the "what" the stakeholders need. It doesn't define "how" this need should be delivered.

When developers examine this requirement, they may initially consider several design options, and then based on risk, time involved, resources available, and other factors, decide upon the best option. In this example, they may consider whether it's better to buy a license for a third-party application or build a new page in the IT solution. The point is, developers have a lot of different considerations at hand when designing the solution that may not be in the minds of stakeholders. At times, developers may request your assistance with design, for example, creating architecture diagrams and screen mockups. Likewise, you may suggest that you could help them in this way also, especially if this is a skillset you can offer. Until you know for certain, do the requirements and leave the design to the developers.

What Are the Different Types of Requirements?

It's useful for you as a business analyst to understand the way in which the *BABOK® Guide* categorizes requirements because other categorization methods exist in other fields. After you've read this material in the *BABOK® Guide*, you'll be in a good position to understand my interpretation of this content:

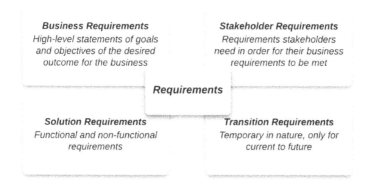

Business Requirements
High-level statements of goals and objectives of the desired outcome for the business

Stakeholder Requirements
Requirements stakeholders need in order for their business requirements to be met

Requirements

Solution Requirements
Functional and non-functional requirements

Transition Requirements
Temporary in nature, only for current to future

Business requirements

Business requirements could be high-level statements of goals and objectives of the desired outcome for the business. They are requirements by and for business stakeholders and are independent of any solution. Many times, business requirements have been defined, even preliminarily, before I'm engaged as a business analyst on the project. An example of an excerpt of a business requirement for the music app is "5% market share."

Stakeholder requirements
Stakeholder requirements are requirements that stakeholders need. Generally, each stakeholder has a unique and distinct interest on your project. Accounting stakeholders don't have the same requirements as health and safety stakeholders (and what kind of a world would we live in if they did!). Typically, stakeholders need their requirements met before the business requirements can be met. An example of an excerpt of a marketing stakeholder requirement for the music app is "adhere to usability standards for apps."

Solution requirements
Solution requirements is where I spend most of my time and it's the main reason that I'm hired. Solution requirements consist of functional and non-functional requirements.

I consider functional requirements the functions (or features, functionality, or behavior) the IT solution must have that the user accesses through the interface; for example, log in, create a playlist, share music, and so on. It answers the question, "What does it do?" If the requirement doesn't involve a user "actively doing something," then I generally classify it as a non-functional requirement.

For me, non-functional requirements are the technical "backend" requirements that tend to be the domain of the developers, such as scalability, speed, availability, response time, and recovery time; for example, "85% of transactions shall be processed within 5 seconds." I don't do a lot of non-functional requirements. There are a couple of reasons for this. One reason is that developers are usually responsible for non-functional requirements. The other reason is that non-functional requirements tend to be standards that are pre-established and reused on projects in the organization.

Transition requirements
Transition requirements are temporary in nature, and assist in advancing the project from current state to future state. Examples include migrating data from the current IT solution to the future IT solution and training personnel on the new IT solution. Both of these examples are "temporary in nature" because after developers migrate the data they're done this major task, and after people are trained on the new system, they don't need to be trained again. In most of the projects I work on, team members don't specifically categorize these requirements as "transition requirements" in the project documentation, but you should be aware of this formal term just in case. Many times, I'm not involved in data migration, but I'm often involved in training personnel on the new IT solution. I may develop formal training material, lead training sessions, or demo the new IT solution as per the stakeholders' needs.

Get RADDical

The Requirements Analysis and Design Definition (RADD) knowledge area from the *BABOK® Guide* is particularly detailed and, dare I say, dense. Don't get me wrong. I actually really like the very precise way that the authors laid out the content; however, day-to-day and in describing this topic to others, I tend to take a simpler approach. First read the *BABOK® Guide* content on RADD, then read this section.

RADD, according to the *BABOK® Guide*, involves "tasks that business analysts perform to structure and organize requirements discovered during elicitation activities, specify and model requirements and designs, validate and verify information, identify solution options that meet business needs, and estimate the potential value that could be realized for each solution option." The *BABOK® Guide* lists the following tasks as part of RADD:

Specify and model requirements: This task refers to analyzing, synthesizing, and refining elicitation results into a visual way to communicate information. In my opinion, while the book says "communicate information" in our context it mostly means writing requirements. Recall, though, that requirements can be represented in different ways such as a diagram, not just written text. For me, it primarily involves creating requirements from the notes I took in stakeholder meetings. Admittedly, most of my requirements are written in text format, but I also do some requirements in a diagram format.

Verify requirements: This task is about ensuring your requirements are usable, consistent, well-written, and can be easily understood by others.

Validate requirements: This task is about ensuring your requirements deliver business value and support the organization's goals and objectives. All requirements must deliver business value; otherwise, why would we have them? Suppose for the music app that some stakeholders would like video capability so that users can have video chats with each other. When the requirements were analyzed for business value, it was determined by the marketing department that most music app users wouldn't use the video capability, so the requirement was deleted.

Define requirements architecture: This task refers to the structure of requirements and how this structure can depict interrelationships among requirements. If you don't have a thoroughly designed way of managing your requirements, your requirements can quickly become a mess! Chaos will descend (I'm not kidding.) The structure you choose needs to clearly depict how requirements are connected to each other. If the organization doesn't have formal requirements architecture tools, I use Microsoft Excel (as I've noted elsewhere) and create a requirements matrix with specific columns that allows me to easily see these interrelationships. For the start-up's music app, requirements could be "flying in" to the business analyst from anywhere, including email or a hallway conversation, so the business analyst would be prudent to find a way to organize the requirements on a scale that's suitable for the start-up.

Define design options: This task refers to exploring design options for the solution approach. For many business analysts working on IT projects, the solution has already been predetermined as an IT solution that is developed in-house or by vendors, or another alternative. For the music app, the app is being developed in-house. If that's the case for your project, you won't be spending a lot of time here.

Analyze potential value and recommend solution: Building on the "define design options" task, this task is about recommending the best solution that delivers the highest value. For many business analysts working on IT projects, the solution has already been predetermined as an IT solution that is developed in-house or by vendors, or another alternative. For the music app, the app is being developed in-house. If that's the case for your project, you won't be spending a lot of time here.

My experience tells me the above tasks are absolutely necessary, but I may do them in a less formal way. My approach may even vary depending on the rigor needed for the project. I'll talk more about all these topics.

Good Versus Bad Requirements

I like the IIBA detail about good, high-quality requirements—a lot. The *BABOK® Guide* says that while quality of requirements is ultimately determined by the needs of stakeholders who use them, high-quality requirements have many of these characteristics: atomic, complete, consistent, concise, feasible, unambiguous, understandable, prioritized, and testable. First read the *BABOK® Guide* then read this section along with the examples in the appendix.

Atomic means "self-contained and capable of being understood independently of other requirements or designs" according to the *BABOK® Guide*. The google dictionary defines atomic as "of or forming a single irreducible unit or component in a larger system." Atoms are really small things. To me, this mean in practical terms that a requirement isn't one big glob of several requirements shoved into one. A requirement needs to be about one thing—one user doing one thing. For the music app, it can be as simple as "user creates profile" or "user updates profile." You wouldn't say "user creates, updates, and deletes profile." This is at least three requirements and isn't atomic. You'll learn more about why atomic requirements are important in the UAT section.

Complete means "enough to guide further work and at the appropriate level of detail for work to continue. The level of completeness required differs based on perspective or methodology, as well as the point in the life cycle where the requirement is being examined or represented" according to the *BABOK® Guide*. To me, this definition is a bit vague, and I'm not sure that I would understand it if I was new to business analysis, but I absolutely agree with "complete" being one of the characteristics of a high-quality requirement. How could you have a requirement that isn't complete? So, for the sake of giving you an example for the music app (which I hope no business analysis ever encounters), if my requirement is "user profiles" I would call that incomplete. What is it about user profiles that we want? Create user profiles? Update user profiles? Delete user profiles? Who is allowed to perform this function? To make this requirement complete, at a minimum include the user, verb and noun; for example, "users need to create profiles." As always, adhere to the standards in your organization.

Consistent means "aligned with the identified needs of the stakeholders and not conflicting with other requirements" according to the *BABOK® Guide*. It's almost a given that your requirements, along with all the rest of your documentation, needs to be consistent. Consistency might mean different things to different people, and some people may be able to strive more towards consistency than others, given their level of skill in writing. It takes a very critical and logical eye to comb through all of the requirements to make sure they are consistent. I spend a lot of my time making requirements consistent. If I already have hundreds of requirements in my requirements matrix, when I add another one weeks later, I need to review the existing requirements to ensure the new ones are consistent and also don't duplicate existing requirements. If you adopt a common writing style and format for your requirements, the consistency check becomes less arduous. You'll save a lot of time if you can write in a consistent way from the beginning of your project. For the music app, if one requirement says, "user creates profile" and another requirement says, "profile is updated by user" then these two formats are inconsistent, and the second should be changed to, "user updates profile."

Concise means "contains no extraneous and unnecessary content," according to the *BABOK® Guide*. Requirements must be concise. Whenever I can, and where there's no loss in meaning, I eliminate words. Requirements shouldn't go on and on and on like a rambling blog post about the intricacies of the perfect apple. Fewer words, ironically, can lead to greater comprehension among your stakeholders because you're more apt to choose your words carefully and stakeholders can focus on the "meat" of what you're saying more easily.

Feasible means "reasonable and possible within the agreed-upon risk, schedule, and budget, or considered feasible enough to investigate further through experiments or prototypes" according to the *BABOK® Guide*. You might have a great requirement, but if it's not feasible, it's no longer a great requirement. In your requirements workshops, you're going to hear a lot of great ideas from stakeholders about the requirements they want. When you continue in your process and put these requirements in front of other stakeholders in project management or IT for approval, you may be told that the requirement is too complex, too expensive to implement, or too risky to consider. This might mean the requirement isn't feasible at this time and can be deferred to a future release, or it may mean the requirement must be deleted. Suppose for the music app that a business stakeholder wants to provide users a link to where they can buy the physical album for that artist; however, upon further investigation the IT stakeholders indicate that doing the coding work for that requirement would delay the project too long, so the requirement is deemed not feasible. A high-quality requirement is one that is also feasible.

Unambiguous means "the requirement must be clearly stated in such a way to make it clear whether a solution does or does not meet the associated need" according to the *BABOK® Guide*. To me, unambiguity is a given. Your requirement needs to be clearly stated in a way that makes it clear whether we should have it as part of the IT solution. Requirements can't be vague. They need to be specific. Anybody who reads the requirement should have a very clear idea about what it means. If some of your stakeholders are asking questions about what the requirement means, this is a very good cue to you that the requirement isn't written as clearly as it needs to be. For the music app, a requirement that says, "search for music" isn't clear enough. Does this mean search filters? Does it mean search for the most popular music? Does it mean search for a specific time period? Does it mean search for music their friends like? Maybe the person who submitted this requirement is clear what "search for music" means, but nobody else is!

Understandable means "represented using common terminology of the audience" according to the *BABOK®*

Guide. When my requirements have the same meaning to *all* of my stakeholders, and they understand the requirements in the same way, then I know I "hit home." This characteristic also alludes to one of the tasks that you need to do when you're in a new environment: learn the terminology of your stakeholders. If one of your stakeholders doesn't understand your requirements, it may be a flag that you're using terminology that isn't typical in that organization. Explain what it means, then ask your stakeholder how it could be reworded to be more understandable. Understandably.

On one project, the large project team comprised of several departmental sub-teams, and each used the word "intake" in different ways to refer to three different tools. For one team, "intake" was the tool used to receive large files, for another team it was the tool used to receive geographical information, and for another team "intake" referred to the method in which an applicant completed an electronic application. When all the sub-teams came together in one room to discuss the entire list of requirements, there was confusion among the stakeholders about what "intake" meant (and it got more confusing when these requirements were sent to the developers).

For the music app, perhaps a stakeholder doesn't understand what a "library" is, so when the requirement says "user needs to add songs to a library," they don't understand because they only know what "library" means in reference to books. If the stakeholder understands that "library" means "everything a user has saved, including playlists, favorite songs and artists," then that stakeholder can understand the requirement in order to be able to approve it.

Prioritized means "ranked, grouped, or negotiated in terms of importance and value against all other requirements" according to the *BABOK® Guide*. On every IT project I've ever worked on, regardless of the software development methodology used, requirements are prioritized. Initially, you may prioritize requirements based on input from stakeholders. After that, you can expect reprioritization to be a continual exercise with stakeholders until—and even after—requirements are passed to developers to code. Developers may indicate that certain requirements are too risky or time-consuming to implement for the next release, and defer them. Various stakeholders of mine have different methods of prioritization that usually centre around perceived business value, so find out what those values are. On an Agile project, requirements are prioritized in the product backlog.

Testable means "able to verify that the requirement or design has been fulfilled. Acceptable levels of verifying fulfillment depend on the level of abstraction of the requirement or design" according to the *BABOK® Guide*. Ouch. I just got a headache. To me, this simply means that requirements need to be written in a way that allows them to be tested and the test either passes or fails (or it can pass with some issues). Can you properly test a requirement that just says "reports required"? No, you can't. But maybe you can test "user creates attendance report," especially if there is acceptance criteria as in the Agile methodology. In the test, the user attempts to create an attendance report. If the user is successful, the test passed; otherwise, the test failed and the functionality failed in the IT solution. Even if you're not involved in testing the IT solution, your requirements need to be written in a manner in which they can be tested. At the very least, the developers need to be able to test the IT solution.

For the music app, suppose the requirement is "user needs to be able to save favorite songs to a library." Suppose also one of the acceptance criteria is "while song is played, user can click the heart, which saves the song in the user's list of favorites." Can this requirement be tested? Yes, it can. The test will verify whether the user can click the heart and save the song. If the song is saved and it shows up in the library, then the test passed.

If a requirement is not atomic, not complete, not consistent, not clear, and not understandable, it may be difficult to test it. If your requirements meet all of these characteristics, then you're well on your way to having the best requirements in town. I'm serious. Be sure to also help your stakeholders understand these characteristics so that your requirements workshops and the entire requirements process will be more productive for you.

Requirements In Agile Methodology

In this book, I've avoided delving into specific software methodologies except for one: Agile. There are several variations of the Agile methodology, and in a general description can be thought of as an expedited method of software development where a version of the working software is created quickly in sprints based on requirements maintained in a product backlog. The working software, which is a smaller subset of functionality, is given to users for immediate feedback. The product backlog is continually mined and reprioritized as requirements are implemented or the priority changes. There is a lot of information about Agile online; nonetheless, as a business analyst you need to understand how that organization is using Agile and what your specific role is, which may not be the "official" way that Agile is intended.

Requirements are written as user stories with acceptance criteria. User stories represent what stakeholders need to do in the IT solution while acceptance criteria are criteria that must be met in order to achieve stakeholder acceptance. Acceptance criteria allow you to create a test for the user story to ensure it was implemented properly. Regardless of whether you're involved in the testing effort, you should do acceptance criteria so you know you're writing good requirements that can be used effectively downstream by other stakeholders such as developers.

User stories are written in business, not technical language, and represent the stakeholders' view of what users need to do. User stories are short, specific, and user-centric. The format for a user story is: As a [user type], I need to [do action] so that I can [goal]. Here's an example:

- **User story:** As an accounting clerk, I need to email customers invoices so they can be billed for work.

This user story is very clear about who needs the functionality, why, and what the goal is. Each user story has acceptance criteria which provides more information about how this user story needs to be implemented. Acceptance criteria also allow us to test if the requirement was implemented properly. Here's an example of acceptance criteria for the above user story:

- **Acceptance criteria:** Accounting clerk accesses the billing page and can successfully create and email an invoice to a customer. Customer receives email, clicks on invoice hyperlink which prompts them to log into their account; the invoice displays on the customer's screen.

Notice how the acceptance criteria provides more detail to support the user story. Without it, developers wouldn't know which page should have this functionality, who the invoice is sent to, and what the format is (that is, a hyperlink). The acceptance criteria and the user story together provide a clear understanding in business language to the developers for further discussion.

Together with the developers you'll identify fields that are needed on the screen at what point in the process (that is, the user workflow) this page shall be available to the user. You'll also specify more information about the requirement, such as identify other roles that need to have permission to send customers invoices, when users should and shouldn't be allowed to send invoices, and so on. Sometimes my new stakeholders (if they're not in IT) are incredulous about how long it takes to do requirements until they do their first project.

For the music app, suppose the user story is "user needs to be able to save favorite songs to a library." The acceptance criteria that will allow this user story to be tested is, "while song is played, user can click the heart, which saves the song in the user's list of favorites." (There can also be several other acceptance criteria.)

There are lots of examples of user stories and acceptance criteria online if you need them, and some examples are also provided in the appendix. Certainly, there is the "perfect" way to do Agile; however, your exact Agile methodology will depend on the environment you're working in. You would be wise to consult with your stakeholders and have a common understanding about their approach to Agile so you can organize your work accordingly.

Help! My Stakeholders Don't "Get" Requirements

It can be a difficult situation when your business stakeholders don't understand requirements nor have IT experience. They may assume that developers can change requirements "on the fly" in the IT solution, not understanding that a small five-second change in the requirements matrix could take a week to change in the IT solution.

I think the biggest problem is that business stakeholders and developers don't understand one another. Business stakeholders may seem unreasonable in their demands to developers, and developers may seem unreasonable in their resistance to impromptu changes from business stakeholders. Business analysts are the glue between the two, to bridge the gap, facilitate a common understanding, and get an IT solution launched! You need to help the entire project team understand more about your world of requirements before the project begins, such as through a meeting. Prior to the meeting, I'd recommend you baseline their knowledge and experience, identify their gaps, and get prepared to teach them what you know so everybody understands requirements in the same way. I may also use a canned presentation I developed that defines the different types of requirements and how to create them.

Be Organized for Your Stakeholders

I try to be organized at every point of the project and in every interaction with stakeholders. Being organized is noticed by stakeholders because it tells them that you value their time. Many business stakeholders are senior people, such as managers, directors and even the executive. The more organized you are, the more you're showing you respect their time and oddly enough, the more time they give you.

Prepare for Your Requirements Workshop

Sometimes new business analysts are intimidated by the term "requirements workshop." For me, "requirements workshop" just means a meeting with a purpose to elicit requirements—to get into the brains of your stakeholders and hear what they want to have as new functionality. Sometimes knowing the way *not* to hold a stakeholder requirements workshop is as good as information about *how* to hold one. Here's what *not* to do:

- Don't send email invitations that don't contain any information—nothing about the topic, what stakeholders need to do before the meeting, or what they need to do in the meeting.
- Don't herd everybody into a room and jump into requirements without setting the stage of the workshop.
- Don't expect people to understand what a requirement is.

Now let's talk about what you *can* do. Prior to the requirements workshop:

Identify stakeholders: Identify the stakeholders and how they'll be grouped into which requirements workshop. You may have stakeholders from several areas including marketing, business, IT, health and safety, and quality assurance. Very rarely do I throw everybody into a room at the same time with all of their varied interests and at a minimum, I'll separate managers from everybody else for the simple reason that managers have different pressures and needs that I should consider, and the personnel seem to feel more comfortable voicing their opinions when their manager isn't sitting beside them. If needed, I'll have one-on-ones with some stakeholders due to their availability or their seniority, or their amount of influence on the project.

Send invitation: Send email invitations according to stakeholder groups. The email invitation should clearly state the purpose of the workshop and include any materials they should review in advance. Most times, I tell stakeholders there is no prep required, but I look forward to their active involvement in the discussion to elicit requirements for the IT solution. The tone of my email is welcoming but professional.

Track invitation responses: Track whether stakeholders have accepted your email invitation. If they declined the invitation, follow-up and ask them when they're available so you can meet with them. I'm willing to go to great lengths to get participation because I know through experience that higher participation rates lead to better results and higher-quality requirements. If a stakeholder can't attend my workshop, then I'll open up my calendar and adjust my schedule to theirs. You don't want to find out the day of your requirements workshop that half of the stakeholders won't be there. Not only do I track their responses, but I also informally verbally confirm with them if I happen to see them casually.

Create workshop presentation: Create a PowerPoint presentation that details the agenda for the workshop. It outlines the project scope, project goals, objectives of the presentation (to elicit requirements as the output), roles and responsibilities, and the format of the workshop. This presentation may only be a few slides long. If this is a first workshop with new stakeholders, then I may also give my canned presentation about what requirements are.

Create notes template: Create a template in which you can populate requirements and notes quickly. I prefer taking my own notes rather than rely on a scribe because I like to nuance my notes and insert private comments, but that's up to you. I've also developed my own electronic "shorthand" consisting of abbreviations and acronyms for diff words and req, uh, I mean, different words and requirements.

Decide techniques: Decide whether you'll be using any other *BABOK® Guide* techniques and prepare templates for those as needed (if the templates don't exist); for example, processes, glossaries, and so on depending on the needs of the project.

Check online attendance: For stakeholders who aren't able to attend in-person, check if they can attend online. I don't like online requirements workshops because it's too easy for stakeholders to be distracted remotely, but on some projects, it's the best that we can do. Video is better than by phone alone.

Lead Your Requirements Workshop

Over time, you're going to develop your own style about how you want to lead your requirements workshops. If you don't have your own style yet, try the following:

- Welcome everybody in the room. Be professional but not stiff or too informal. Your tone will set the tone of the room, and I like the room to have a light tone where people feel comfortable to speak their mind and excited to be engaged.
- If stakeholders are new to each other, do a round of introductions.
- Review the PowerPoint presentation that describes the objectives of today's workshop and the output that you need. I'm very welcoming in my tone and tell stakeholders that I want to hear their vision for the project. If they could have their wish list of requirements, what would it look like?
- Review the canned PowerPoint presentation that defines what a requirement is, if needed.
- Review the "ground rules" of the workshop, which may include describing your role and the roles of the stakeholders. I like to explain that while I'm facilitating, I'm also writing notes, so it's important that stakeholders are mindful of the slower pace I need for my multitasking. This point also helps stakeholders understand that talking over each other or at the same time isn't effective.
- Work through the agenda items and take notes in your template. I don't share my raw notes with stakeholders (because I take electronic shorthand and may also write private comments), but I do let them

know I'll be sending a workshop summary to them. In my notes, I document risks, potential problems, requirements, action items (with the person responsible and date required), and other information.

- At the end of the workshop, I thank everybody for attending and acknowledge the valuable time they took out of their day (because it's true).

Tips for Taking Notes in a Requirements Workshop

Requirements workshops are my main source of information for creating requirements. Sometimes the discussion moves really quickly. If I didn't have efficient methods of capturing a fast-paced discussion, I might lose some of these valuable stakeholder comments. One way that I keep up is by taking electronic shorthand. If you're interested, here is some of my shorthand:

- ACT = action needed (by somebody)
- dead = deadline
- dep = depends or dependency
- diff = different
- dis = discussion occurring
- eg = for example
- F = functional requirement
- fu = follow-up
- fut = future
- IT = IT department or person in room
- NB = important
- NF = non-functional requirement

- proj = project
- R = risk
- req = requirement
- sol = solution
- U = you
- UR = you are

I insert stakeholder initials beside their comment (for traceability) and if the stakeholder or myself also has an action item, I'll indicate it as "JIM DO" or "PAM DO." Using electronic shorthand allows me to categorize information as I go, and since I'm using consistent notation as I type, I can easily search my notes later, collect the information, and transfer it into the requirements matrix. I'm rarely able to capture the final form of a requirement in these meetings because it takes several iterations for me to wordsmith the requirement, verify and validate with stakeholders, and have it approved. Taking notes in an efficient, streamlined way has the added benefit of using less of stakeholders' time during requirements creation and maintenance, which is also appreciated.

Encourage Participation in a Requirements Workshop

Stakeholders are busy, tired, and not interested. I get this. They have too much work and not enough time. Sometimes it's difficult to get stakeholders interested in participating in requirements workshops, yet they are critical to a business analyst's success. There are lots of methods I use to help engage stakeholders.

First of all, the more positive and appreciative that I am, the more that I comment on stakeholders' discussion in a positive way that shows I value their participation, the more they talk. I also use nonverbal cues to keep them talking, like nodding my head and typing. The quieter I am, the more they talk. Maybe they're uncomfortable with silence and don't like the dead air. Whatever the reason, the less I talk, the more they talk, and the more information I get.

Second, contrary to logic, stakeholders don't mind if you interrupt them while they're talking—if the intent of your interruption is to clarify their comments. They appreciate that you care enough to hear them properly. I interrupt sparingly, but when I do, it seems to be an effective tool to get more information.

Third, I don't argue. In an initial workshop, I don't argue with anything the stakeholder says. I don't say "that requirement isn't possible" or "I doubt we can do that" or "your expectations are too unrealistic" (even if they are). I let it all come tumbling out. At this point, it's important for me to focus on building the relationship and encouraging participation by active listening.

Appreciate that Your Stakeholders are Different

Not everybody is the same, right? We know this. We hear information with our own built-in bias based on our experience in this world. We come from different cultures. English might be our second language. We may have a learning disability. We may be introverted or extroverted. We may absorb information visually, not verbally. We're just plain different, right? The more you recognize this, the more successful your projects will be.

Of course we're different, you might say. That's as obvious as a wood floor has wood. So it is. But what does this mean in practical, day-to-day terms for you as a business analyst? I worked with a project manager who was clearly an auditory learner. She liked the verbal banter of meetings, preferred spoken instructions, and liked discussion. She moved the meeting along at a very quick pace, not waiting for anybody to write down notes or map ideas on a whiteboard because she didn't need it. She didn't pause in between concepts and check in with the group to see what their thoughts were, nor verify if they absorbed the concepts she was communicating. She didn't solicit feedback along the way, nor did she want to. She assumed that everybody learned like she did and since she believed she was communicating clearly, she also assumed everybody understood.

This project manager neglected to consider that not everybody in the room was an auditory learner. I'm primarily a visual learner, which means that I remember best what I can see—pictures work well for me. So do demos, movies, and flowcharts. I write words down. I take extensive notes, but in this meeting, which ran as fast as an ant from a sneaker, I could barely take any. When this project manager turned to me at the end of the meeting and said, "Did you get all that?" I faltered. Get all what?

Given my teaching background, in my meetings I try to engage as many of the learning styles as I can, and at a minimum, present the same information in both verbal and visual ways. If I'm on stage presenting, I'll also incorporate kinesthetic methods. It's said that most technical people are visual learners. They need information presented visually, or they might just hear "blah, blah, blah" like I did, and retain very little. Since I'm introverted, I appreciate the need of introverts to "go away from the meeting and think about it" before they give their final comments. It doesn't help my project if I only think about my own communication and learning style.

Get to know your stakeholders and morph yourself in a way that encourages their highest participation. People want to contribute and feel heard, and they'll talk more if you go the extra step to make them feel comfortable. A business analyst without active and engaged stakeholders is going nowhere, so appreciate that your stakeholders are different.

The Day After a Requirements Workshop

After you've survived your requirements workshop, send an email to attendees to thank them for coming to the workshop, and also provide a summary of action items. Next, transfer your notes into a requirements matrix. As previously indicated, you can use Excel or another tool of your choice. You may also want to create other deliverables in discussion with stakeholders based on the techniques that you've selected for your project. When your requirements matrix is ready for their review, set up additional requirements workshops to review the accuracy and completeness of the requirements you captured and also to elicit new requirements.

Dealing with Difficult Stakeholders

When I'm on a job interview, I'm often asked, "How do you deal with difficult stakeholders?" Eyes seem to light up when I say, "In my mind, there aren't difficult stakeholders, just difficult situations." Whichever way you want to look at the ball, there *are* difficulties involving stakeholders on projects.

What can you do about difficult stakeholders? The stakeholder who knocks you and other stakeholders down and monopolizes the entire meeting just because he enjoys hearing his own words. The bull. The tarantula. The lion. On one hand, you don't want to alienate a stakeholder who might be a valuable resource for you but on the other hand, if you're having meeting after meeting and not getting the information you need, your own deadlines are at risk. When I had a stakeholder like this, I approached him privately and said, "You have so much knowledge that I'm finding it impossible to capture all of it in a single meeting. Would you be open to me setting up additional meetings with you?" Of course he was, and I was able to take him out of the main meeting without offending him.

I also worked on a project where nobody liked the director, and didn't care if his IT solution failed (having worked with him, I understood their feelings). In the beginning when I worked with them, there was clear apathy and disinterest in the project. I was barely getting any requirements at all. What did I do? Instead of moving away from these stakeholders, I l-e-a-n-e-d into them. I leaned hard. I made an extra effort to get to know them, professional and personally, and develop a solid, productive relationship with them. I tried to create a positive presence, showed interest and appreciation for their work, and actively listened to their concerns. I tried to empathize with their perspectives and understand their point of view. One by one, I was able to develop the rapport that I needed to understand their needs and create the requirements.

Another type of difficult situation can be when stakeholders disagree. They're people, and people disagree. So what can you do about it as a business analyst? It's quite understandable that stakeholders have disagreements about requirements to be implemented because there's only a finite amount of time and money to develop the IT solution. Every stakeholder, understandably, wants to advance their own interests; however, decisions must be made based on business value and the goals of the project for the organization.

In my view, the first step to resolving stakeholder disagreements is to understand each stakeholder's perspectives. Empathize with their points of view. Hear them out and reflect back to them what your understanding is about their positions. Clarify their comments as needed and write them down so they know you're taking it seriously. Eventually, as a team, you may come to a "natural" consensus (especially if there's an executive in the room); otherwise, you may want to park it for a later time.

For one particularly heated debate, I parked it, then created a small PowerPoint that outlined the options, as well as the benefits and risks. When I presented the information to the stakeholders I also invited a higher-ranking manager and the decision was made immediately. In my experience, disagreements among stakeholders are healthy, and much healthier than apathy. Encourage people to be passionate and have mechanisms to deal with the dissent.

What Is Requirements Life Cycle Management?

Requirements Life Cycle Management (RLCM) knowledge area, as detailed in the *BABOK® Guide*, is about managing and maintaining requirements from inception to retirement. Requirements have a relatively long life cycle. You create them early in the project, update them as needed with the stakeholders, hand them over to the developers for coding, and then possibly update them again. You may delete some along the way.

During testing (such as UAT) you'll revisit them again to make sure the requirements are represented in the IT solution, then at the end of the project, you'll be finished with them. They've done their job and are retired!

It's critical that you have ways to manage requirements throughout the RLCM. I think of requirements as an intricate "spider web" of interdependencies. When one changes, you need to carefully and analytically examine all the other requirements for updating, deferring, or deleting. Retired requirements on one project may be used on future projects, so that's another reason that RLCM is so important. These requirements can be tagged for future use and removed from consideration from your current project. You can save time and have consistency among projects.

The treatment of RLCM in the *BABOK® Guide* is excellent, and upon reading it, you may have a real appreciation for the thoroughness of the *BABOK® Guide*. In it, you'll see that RLCM has five main tasks:

Trace requirements: This task is about analyzing and maintaining the relationships between requirements, designs, solution components, and so on. To me, this means you're able to trace the life of that requirement, much like a person's life, from birth to death. You know where they've been, how they've changed, and what they've done. You know what their relationships are to other people around them and how they impact each other. You must always have the ability, at any point in the life cycle, to be able to identify the state and content of the requirement at that time. If somebody asks, "When did that requirement get deleted and why?" you should be able to find that information easily. Likewise if the requirement was updated, deferred, or retired. There are formal business analysis tools you can use for traceability, but if you don't have them, you can dedicate a column(s) in your requirements matrix for this purpose.

Maintain requirements: This task is about ensuring requirements are accurate and current throughout the RLCM in a way that facilitates reuse. Makes sense, right? Note that if you created good, high-quality requirements, then your requirements are more prone to inherently facilitating reuse.

Prioritize requirements: This task is about ranking requirements in the order of relative importance, initially and throughout the RLCM until the requirement is implemented by developers. Prioritization is a continual process, from the moment I step into a stakeholder meeting to the instant I give the requirements to developers. It's an exercise that inevitably everybody on the project team will have a say in, whether you like it or not, based on perceived benefit, cost, risk, time sensitivity, regulatory compliance, and other factors (sometimes it's just about ego!).

Assess requirements changes: This task is about evaluating the implications of proposed changes to requirements. Requirements (and information related to them, such as their status and priority) are always changing … always. Even after they're approved by stakeholders, you'll need to continue updating them for a variety of reasons. Keeping in mind that requirements are really an interconnected spider web and moving, changing, or breaking one strand could affect the others, it's critical that you have a structured process for assessing requirements changes, not change requirements in an erratic and unpredictable, undocumented way. In my requirements matrix, in the notes column, I have every change clearly documented—when, by who, and why. If I reject a proposed change, I also document that. Changes to requirements can literally come from anywhere—an email from a stakeholder, a hallway conversation, or another source. For each change, we need to apply our requirements change process to critically analyze it for benefit (versus risk or cost) and other factors. Changes can be approved as is, approved with modifications, or rejected. Know and understand your organization's approach to change, which may vary among projects.

Approve requirements: This task is literally what it says—requirements approvals. Inevitably, you're going to develop your own approval processes on your projects within the framework of your organization's approach to approvals, including the role of your stakeholders. Nonetheless, I also talk about some ideas with respect to approvals in this book.

Keep Your Requirements Clean

You need a process for maintaining your requirements and making changes, even if you're the only person who has access to the requirements matrix. You don't want the requirements matrix to be a "free for all" for changes by anybody, including yourself. You'll want changes signed off formally (or informally, as per your organization), and be careful of accepting unilateral changes from any one stakeholder unless there's a clear understanding among stakeholders about who the owner (and authority) is for a set of requirements. Sometimes organizations may also require a strict change management process for requirements, especially if the requirements are for an IT solution that is already in production. In my Excel requirements matrix, I include all relevant comments along with the date I received them. If anybody asks me anything about any requirement of theirs at any point in the life cycle, I'm able to respond. It shows that you're organized, professional, and you take your job seriously.

Delete Your Requirements

When can you delete a requirement? The short answer to this might be "never"! I say this partly as a joke, of course, because what I mean is that you always need to have traceability, even for requirements that stakeholders don't want anymore. At any given time, you need to be able to go into your requirements matrix and find the history of that requirement, even if it was deleted a year ago. If I don't have a dedicated requirements tool and I'm using Excel, to keep my requirements matrix clean, I use strikeout font and change the status column to "deleted". I'll even distinguish between statuses of "deleted not needed" or "deleted IT can't do" because I want to track these differences over time.

Get Your Requirements Approved

Requirements approval—the how, who, what, and when—varies among organizations and even among projects. It can be formal or informal and is an ongoing process. You need to approve not only the requirement itself, but information related to the requirement, such as state, category, planned release version, and so on (meaning, the columns in your requirements matrix). You may need your requirements approved by one stakeholder or many, and keep track of who approved what and when. I use my requirements matrix (the notes column and some other columns) to track all of this if I don't have an alternate tool.

Most likely your requirements don't need approval from all of your stakeholders. It's part of developing your approval process to determine which stakeholders will be approving which requirements, and the method they'll be using; for example, an email, meeting, or formal signoff. When there are conflicts among stakeholders, it's your job as a business analyst to resolve them.

For my projects, after the business stakeholders approve the requirements (preferably in requirements workshops, where I step through each requirement and what it means), then I meet with the developers. Just because the business has approved the requirements matrix doesn't mean it will be the final list of requirements, since developers have very different perspectives on the same requirements due to several factors, including technology constraints, resourcing, timelines, other projects in the cue, and budgets.

In this meeting with developers and with the product owner (or other key business stakeholder) I step through each requirement (much like I did when seeking business approval) and we examine it from the developer perspective. This is a very different conversation than the one I would have had with business stakeholders, which is why I have separate meetings.

It's really key to listen to the concerns of developers and try to understand their world because ultimately, you need to get into their development schedule (not the other way around). It's very possible that by listening and responding to their needs and earnestly getting to know them as a stakeholder that concessions you're willing to do for priority or scope could facilitate a stronger relationship with developers and they would be willing to be receptive to the same flexibility when you need it. I often find that the more I avoid the hardline approach with developers, the better results I get (as it's said, "more bees with honey"). It might mean that some functionality is deferred to another release, modified to reduce the scope, or omitted in favor of a manual workaround.

Certainly, we can't compromise high-priority functionality. We can't compromise on hard deadlines that the organization is expected to adhere to, for regulatory or other sound business reasons, but where I can be flexible, I am. Maybe it's possible to implement half of a requirement in the next version, and the rest of it in a subsequent release. Maybe we can change a requirement so that it can be done easier and faster by developers, thus saving them time. Maybe we can use a third-party application the developers can integrate with the IT solution, rather than asking developers to start coding from scratch. The third-party application has been thoroughly tested and is "ready to go" because it's already available to consumers. Why not use it, if we can and it's not problematic?

During this meeting, in my requirements matrix I typically add developers' feedback and the decision in a column dedicated for this meeting, which I call "IT feedback." I take notes the same way I always do, in consistent notation that allows me to easily search for terms later. If there are any problematic issues that need to be brought back to business stakeholders, they can be easily searched for. When I debrief business stakeholders about developers' feedback, I always try to present developers in a positive light in the spirit of collaboration. Positivity is a contagious thing, and a positive team environment helps in every way on a project.

How User Acceptance Testing Affects Requirements

This book isn't about User Acceptance Testing (UAT) but it's worthwhile to show you how your hard work in developing high-quality requirements pays off near the end of the project in UAT.

As developers get closer to finishing the release, before they're allowed to release the system into production they'll need signoff by business stakeholders that the system has their requested requirements and it's working as business stakeholders need it to. This is known as UAT. As a business analyst, you may participate or even lead the UAT efforts.

Prior to UAT, and preferably at the beginning of your project, you'll define your UAT process with your business stakeholders so they know what to expect months later. Some organizations don't have defined UAT processes, and the UAT testers (who are select business stakeholders assigned to do UAT) aren't given any guidance about how to test the system. I've encountered many organizations that do UAT this way, in an unstructured "free-for-all" like a rush to a cheap buffet. They bang away recklessly at the system trying to find defects and are lucky if they find any.

I recommend a structured approach to UAT where you create UAT tests for all the requirements. Over time, you'll know which tests you can omit (perhaps because doing one test allows you to cover multiple requirements) but for now assume that you need to do a test for every requirement. You'll also need a defined and structured way of documenting and communicating defects to developers. Hopefully this is a process you developed in consultation with developers at the beginning of your project.

Now, in UAT, you'll understand why it was so important that you created high-quality requirements. Suppose the business analyst wrote low-quality or incomplete requirements, or wrote a requirement that actually represented multiple functions (I've seen this, by the way, where stakeholders globbed together multiple requirements into one because they didn't apply the concept of "atomic"). How can the UAT team develop a test for that requirement when it's actually several requirements? Which requirement is it actually testing, and what about the others? If the test failed, how would they know what part of the requirement failed, if the requirement was actually several functions globbed together?

If the business analyst wrote low-quality and incomplete requirements, now the UAT team can only develop low-quality, incomplete and/or faulty tests. Suppose also the business analyst didn't develop an effective requirements architecture, so now the requirements matrix is a mess and it's difficult to know which requirements were already implemented on a prior release, which ones need to be tested, and which ones could be omitted from testing because the functionality was tested as part of another requirement to save time in testing.

If you're tasked with creating UAT tests, know that the acceptance criteria you did can easily form the basis for the test, so you don't need to spend a lot of extra time developing the testing document. Remember, when the acceptance criteria are met in the IT solution, then that signifies business stakeholders are satisfied and willing to sign off on that requirement.

If you have low-quality requirements, then you'll have a low-quality UAT, business users will sign off on a low-quality system, and developers will release a low-quality system into production. That's a big headache for everybody and an immense waste of resources throughout the project. Take the time to do high-quality requirements so you can have a successful UAT.

Communication, Communication, Communication

I once heard an excellent project manager say there are three factors in a successful project: communication, communication, and communication. He was right.

I spent the first five years of my career in communications. It was so interesting to me that communications wasn't common sense to everybody, that senders of communication just sent verbal rambling run-ons as "communication" to receivers, or stakeholders, and they didn't take the time to design the information before they sent it. Did I say design? Yes, I did. Information must be designed for the intended audience based on your message, information to be understood, assumptions, and base level of knowledge of the recipient.

For example, some senders might be pressed for time and rationalize that sending out rambling information that contained too much information for one part of the audience and not enough for the others, was justified. After all, at least they get the information, right? The reality is, if you don't take the time to craft your message properly, using the right medium or technique then maybe nobody read or understood it.

Marshall McLuhan's comment in his 1964 book *Understanding Media: The Extensions of Man,* still has relevance today: "the medium is the message." It means that the method in which a message is sent (print, visual, and so on) determines the ways in which that message will be perceived. As business analysts, we want to choose the right technique to deliver our messages, and ideally, use information design principles to guide our reader. If our readers are saying "I missed that because the information was embedded in a bunch of text" or, "I didn't see it because it was on the second page" then we need to take another look at how we structure and communicate information.

Hand in hand with McLuhan's sage words are the business analysis techniques we choose to communicate information. If we present 200 requirements to executives at one of their meetings for approval, we're likely not to get very far; however, if we summarize those two hundred requirements into a 20-minute presentation, we're likely to get the approval we're seeking. It sounds counter-intuitive, doesn't it, that *not* presenting all the information actually gets us the approval we're seeking? The higher in the organization you go, the less detail and the more summaries you need.

I'd love to do an entire book about this, because I've seen how information design can really "make or break" successful communication and whether messages are clearly understood. Remember what a wise project manager told me about the three factors needed for a successful project: communication, communication, and communication.

Appendix: Sample List of Requirements

This appendix provides a sample list of requirements in the Agile format. These examples only represent one way of creating requirements. As mentioned elsewhere, check with your organization, especially with your IT stakeholders, about acceptable requirements formats for your project. The best way to create good requirements is to have examples of ones that already have that stamp of approval from the organization.

Requirements are more effective if written in the active voice, including the role, verb, and main noun (for example, "accounting clerk sends invoices"). This structure also enables you to easily generate more requirements with different verbs, such as "update," "view," "delete," "approve," and so on. Below are some examples of requirements in the Agile format:

Example 1. User story: As an accounting clerk, I need to email customers invoices so they can be billed for work. **Acceptance criteria:** Accounting clerk accesses the billing page and can successfully create and email an invoice to a customer. Customer receives email, clicks on invoice hyperlink which prompts them to log into their account; the invoice displays on the customer's screen.

Example 2. User story: As a user, I need to update my profile name so my profile is accurate. **Acceptance criteria:** User successfully updates name on profile page.

Example 3. User story: As a user, I need to change my password. **Acceptance criteria:** User accesses their profile, on the menu clicks password, then changes password. Password is changed.

Example 4. User story: As a manager, I need to generate a report about staff who were sick. **Acceptance criteria:** Manager accesses the reports module and generates a report about staff who were sick. Report shows sick staff in daily, weekly, and monthly views. Report can be sorted by staff first or last name. Report can be exported to Excel.

Example 5. User story: As a student, I need to register for a course so I can attend class. **Acceptance criteria:** Student accesses the registration page and can successfully register for desired course. Student receives confirmation of registration by email.

About the Author

Pamela Paterson, MS, CBAP, is an IT business analyst, teacher, author, and speaker. She is a dedicated mentor to those who strive for positive change in their lives, and with this aim in mind has written several books including an international best-seller. She enjoys collaborating on writing projects with like-minded people. Pamela is based in Kingston, Ontario, Canada.

Acknowledgements

Without the dedicated staff at IIBA, this book would not be possible. I owe my special thanks for the excellent content in the *BABOK® Guide* to business analysts and other collaborators throughout the world. My special thanks to Paul Stapleton from the IIBA for his expedited and detailed comments and support of the book. My sincere appreciation to my husband Tarek Hussein and friend Tala Farag for reviewing the book and making very thoughtful suggestions that improved the quality of the content.

Share Your Thoughts

Do you have business analysis tips that work for you? Share your thoughts. Contact me on Twitter @pampaterson.

www.ingramcontent.com/pod-product-compliance
Lightning Source LLC
Chambersburg PA
CBHW031229050326